WHSmith

Challenge Maths
KS2: Year 3
Age 7–8

**Paul Broadbent and
Peter Patilla**

Text and illustrations © Hodder Education

First published in 2007
exclusively for WHSmith by
Hodder Education
338 Euston Road
London NW1 3BH

Impression number   10 9 8 7 6 5 4 3 2 1
Year   2010 2009 2008 2007

Cover illustration by Sally Newton Illustrations

Typeset by Servis Filmsetting Ltd, Manchester

Printed and bound UK by CPI Bath

A CIP record for this book is available from the
British Library

ISBN: 978 0 340 94542 1

Contents

Parents' notes

How this book can help your child

- This book has been written for children who are between 7 and 8 years old.
- It will support and improve the work they are doing at school, whichever Maths scheme they use.
- The activities in the book have been carefully written to include the content expected of children at this stage in their development.
- The activities will help prepare your child for the different types of tests that occur in schools.

Materials needed

- Pencil, coloured pencils, eraser, watch and centimetre ruler.

Using this book

- There are 24 topics and 4 tests in the book. Each test covers 6 topics.
- Each topic is about a week's work.
- Do give help and encouragement. The activities should not be a chore.
- A calculator should not be used for the work in this book.
- Do let your child mark his or her own work under your supervision and correct any careless mistakes they might have made.
- When all the tests have been completed let your child fill in the Certificate of Achievement on the opposite page.
- Each double page has a title, explanation of the learning point, practice section, and challenge section.

Topic – the main learning point

Get started – helpful information and tips about the learning point

Practice – straightforward follow-up to the learning point

Challenge – uses the learning point in a slightly different way and takes it further

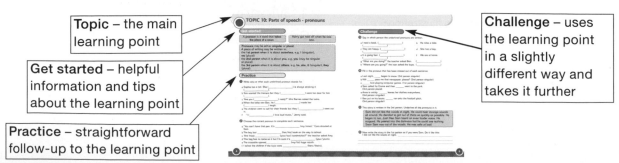

**This certifies
that**

_____

has completed

CHALLENGE MATHS YEAR 3

on _____

Scoring _____ on TEST 1

_____ on TEST 2

_____ on TEST 3

and _____ on TEST 4

**Total score
out of 100** _____

40–50	**good effort**
50–60	**well done**
60–70	**fantastic**
70–100	**brilliant**

Topic 1: Addition facts

Get started

Remember: the order in which you add **does not** matter.

5 + 12 is the same as **12 + 5**   **9 + 7** is the same as **7 + 9**

Here are some addition words that you will come across:

add, total, sum, increase, plus, altogether, more than

This is the addition sign **+**

Practice

1 **Try to answer each block of additions in under 30 seconds.**

a	b	c	d
9 + 8 = ____	8 + 5 = ____	12 + 6 = ____	4 + 13 = ____
7 + 5 = ____	7 + 7 = ____	13 + 4 = ____	6 + 12 = ____
6 + 8 = ____	6 + 9 = ____	11 + 5 = ____	3 + 11 = ____
5 + 7 = ____	6 + 7 = ____	17 + 3 = ____	8 + 12 = ____
9 + 3 = ____	9 + 9 = ____	14 + 6 = ____	5 + 13 = ____
8 + 8 = ____	6 + 6 = ____	15 + 2 = ____	2 + 17 = ____
3 + 7 = ____	8 + 7 = ____	11 + 7 = ____	5 + 15 = ____
6 + 5 = ____	5 + 5 = ____	12 + 4 = ____	7 + 12 = ____
4 + 7 = ____	6 + 5 = ____	16 + 3 = ____	4 + 11 = ____
9 + 2 = ____	9 + 7 = ____	13 + 5 = ____	6 + 14 = ____

2 **Complete these grids.**

a

+	3	7	8
4			
6			
8			

b

+	2	3	5
11			
12			
15			

c

+	12	13	14
4			
5			
6			

Challenge

③ Fill in the missing numbers.

a 8 + ◯ = 12   b 12 + ◯ = 16   c ◯ + 6 = 13   d ◯ + 3 = 18

e 5 + ◯ = 11   f 10 + ◯ = 18   g ◯ + 5 = 12   h ◯ + 5 = 19

i 8 + ◯ = 14   j 14 + ◯ = 20   k ◯ + 9 = 14   l ◯ + 3 = 20

m 6 + ◯ = 15   n 17 + ◯ = 19   o ◯ + 9 = 18   p ◯ + 7 = 18

q 4 + ◯ = 13   r 13 + ◯ = 17   s ◯ + 7 = 12   t ◯ + 4 = 20

④ Write the answers.

a Total 5 and 7 ⟶ ☐   b Add 14 to 4 ⟶ ☐   c Total 3, 6 and 4 ⟶ ☐

d Add 7 to 9 ⟶ ☐   e Increase 13 by 7 ⟶ ☐   f Add 5, 4 and 6 ⟶ ☐

g 8 plus 6 ⟶ ☐   h Total 15 and 4 ⟶ ☐   i Sum 5, 7 and 8 ⟶ ☐

j Increase 8 by 3 ⟶ ☐   k 16 more than 3 ⟶ ☐   l 7 plus 3 plus 8 ⟶ ☐

m 7 more than 5 ⟶ ☐   n 12 plus 5 ⟶ ☐   o Total 7, 7 and 3 ⟶ ☐

⑤ Look at what each machine does to change numbers.
Write the missing numbers in the tables.

a

IN	4		7		14
OUT		10		16	

b

IN	0		5		8
OUT		15		18	

Write what each machine is doing to the numbers.

c

IN	7	8	10	12	15
OUT	11	12	14	16	19

d

IN	0	3	5	6	8
OUT	11	14	16	17	19

Topic 2: Subtraction facts

Get started

Remember: the order in which you subtract **does** matter.

12 − 7 is **not** the same as **7 − 12**

Here are some subtraction words that you will come across:

take, subtract, minus, fewer than, less than, reduce, difference

This is the subtract sign −

Practice

1 Try to answer each block of subtractions in under 30 seconds.

a	b	c	d
13 − 6 = ___	14 − 6 = ___	11 − 9 = ___	10 − 2 = ___
11 − 5 = ___	13 − 9 = ___	12 − 4 = ___	19 − 9 = ___
12 − 5 = ___	12 − 3 = ___	17 − 9 = ___	16 − 9 = ___
11 − 7 = ___	17 − 8 = ___	16 − 7 = ___	12 − 2 = ___
10 − 6 = ___	18 − 9 = ___	15 − 6 = ___	11 − 4 = ___
15 − 8 = ___	16 − 6 = ___	11 − 8 = ___	13 − 3 = ___
12 − 6 = ___	11 − 3 = ___	11 − 7 = ___	14 − 5 = ___
13 − 8 = ___	12 − 8 = ___	12 − 5 = ___	18 − 8 = ___
14 − 7 = ___	13 − 7 = ___	14 − 8 = ___	15 − 9 = ___
16 − 8 = ___	14 − 9 = ___	16 − 8 = ___	13 − 4 = ___

2 Write the difference between each pair of numbers.

a (8)(13) ⟶ ( )   b (20)(13) ⟶ ( )   c (18)(4) ⟶ ( )

d (15)(7) ⟶ ( )   e (11)(18) ⟶ ( )   f (3)(19) ⟶ ( )

g (17)(8) ⟶ ( )   h (16)(12) ⟶ ( )   i (17)(3) ⟶ ( )

j (6)(13) ⟶ ( )   k (11)(16) ⟶ ( )   l (20)(6) ⟶ ( )

Challenge

3 Fill in the missing numbers.

a $12 - \bigcirc = 8$ b $17 - \bigcirc = 14$ c $\bigcirc - 4 = 9$ d $\bigcirc - 5 = 12$

e $12 - \bigcirc = 5$ f $19 - \bigcirc = 11$ g $\bigcirc - 6 = 6$ h $\bigcirc - 3 = 14$

i $15 - \bigcirc = 8$ j $14 - \bigcirc = 12$ k $\bigcirc - 8 = 5$ l $\bigcirc - 8 = 11$

m $11 - \bigcirc = 4$ n $20 - \bigcirc = 13$ o $\bigcirc - 9 = 7$ p $\bigcirc - 3 = 16$

q $17 - \bigcirc = 9$ r $18 - \bigcirc = 16$ s $\bigcirc - 5 = 8$ t $\bigcirc - 8 = 12$

4 Write the answers.

a 15 subtract 8 ⟶ ☐ b 8 less than 18 ⟶ ☐ c 20 minus 13 ⟶ ☐

d 16 minus 7 ⟶ ☐ e Subtract 3 from 14 ☐ f Subtract 13 from 18 ➤ ☐

g 11 take away 3 ⟶ ☐ h Take 5 from 20 ⟶ ☐ i Reduce 19 by 16 ⟶ ☐

j Decrease 14 by 5 ➤ ☐ k 19 minus 3 ⟶ ☐ l Decrease 16 by 10 ➤ ☐

m Reduce 13 by 7 ➤ ☐ n 17 decreased by 4 ➤ ☐ o 11 less than 17 ⟶ ☐

5 Write + or − in each star to make the number sentences true.

a

$8 ★ 9 ★ 3 = 14$

b

$8 ★ 8 ★ 2 = 2$

c

$9 ★ 4 ★ 2 = 11$

d

$6 ★ 2 ★ 9 = 13$

e

$5 ★ 5 ★ 4 = 6$

f

$7 ★ 9 ★ 3 = 13$

g

$8 ★ 5 ★ 3 = 16$

h

$9 ★ 4 ★ 2 = 3$

i

$6 ★ 5 ★ 9 = 2$

Topic 3: Place value

Numbers are built up using **digits**.

There are ten **digits** 0, 1, 2, 3, 4, 5, 6, 7, 8 and 9.

The number 6475 is a four-digit number that uses the four **digits** 6, 4, 7 and 5.

The position of a **digit** in a number gives its value.

$$6475 = 6000 + 400 + 70 + 5$$

thousands hundreds tens units

Practice

1 **Use digits to write these numbers.**

a eight hundred and fifty _____

b one thousand, two hundred _____

c three hundred and three _____

d three thousand and eighty _____

e nine hundred and sixty-seven _____

f six thousand and twelve _____

g five hundred and fifteen _____

h seven thousand and four _____

i seven hundred and twenty-five _____

j nine thousand, two hundred and thirty six _____

2 **Write these answers as three-digit numbers.**

a 400 + 70 + 8 = _____   b 200 + 30 + 2 = _____

c 700 + 90 + 7 = _____   d 100 + 40 + 5 = _____

e 800 + 30 + 3 = _____   f 500 + 50 + 6 = _____

g 900 + 20 + 1 = _____   h 300 + 10 + 4 = _____

3 Write these three-digit numbers in hundreds, tens and units.

a 436 = _____ + _____ + _____   b 184 = _____ + _____ + _____

c 662 = _____ + _____ + _____   d 715 = _____ + _____ + _____

e 938 = _____ + _____ + _____   f 541 = _____ + _____ + _____

g 253 = _____ + _____ + _____   h 897 = _____ + _____ + _____

Challenge

4 The arrows point to digits. Write what the digits are worth.

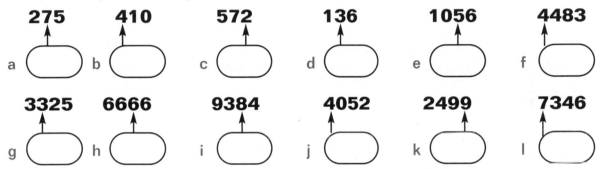

5 Write these numbers in order, starting with the smallest.

a 150   105   501   510   550   505   b 763   376   673   367   736   637

_____ _____ _____ _____ _____ _____   _____ _____ _____ _____ _____ _____

c 238   832   823   283   328   382   d 1234   3421   4123   1432   3124

_____ _____ _____ _____ _____ _____   _____ _____ _____ _____ _____

e 2074   7024   2704   2407   4270   f 2010   1002   1200   1020   2100

_____ _____ _____ _____ _____   _____ _____ _____ _____ _____

6 Arrange these three digits to make six different numbers.   **4, 5 and 7**

_____ _____ _____ _____ _____ _____

Write the numbers in order, starting with the smallest.

Topic 4: Counting

Get started

Use your counting skills to help you add or subtract numbers in your head.

Adding and subtracting small numbers

Count on or back ————→ 187 + 5 = 192   281 − 4 = 277

Count on from the smaller to
the larger number ————————————→

The <u>difference</u> between
245 and 251 is 6

Adding and subtracting 9

To add 9, add on 10
then count back 1

176 + 9 ———→

To subtract 9, take away
10 then count on 1

153 − 9 ———→

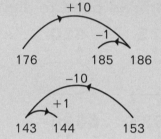

Practice

1 **Answer these as quickly as you can.**

a 35 +5 ◯   b 69 +3 ◯   c 48 +6 ◯   d 77 +8 ◯

e 42 −4 ◯   f 64 −5 ◯   g 72 −8 ◯   h 84 −6 ◯

i 127 +4 ◯   j 189 +2 ◯   k 608 +3 ◯   l 799 +5 ◯

m 172 −3 ◯   n 512 −7 ◯   o 643 −6 ◯   p 804 −5 ◯

2 **Work these out in your head.**

a Write the differences.

67 74 ——→ ◯

91 88 ——→ ◯

145 152 ——→ ◯

473 467 ——→ ◯

b Add on 9.

78 ——→ ◯

94 ——→ ◯

286 ——→ ◯

698 ——→ ◯

c Subtract 9.

77 ——→ ◯

92 ——→ ◯

304 ——→ ◯

445 ——→ ◯

Challenge

3 Write what the darts are doing to the numbers. Continue the chains.

the rule is

a 16 ▻— 26 ▻— 36 ▻— ◯ ▻— ◯ ▻— ◯ | |

the rule is

b 33 ▻— 37 ▻— 41 ▻— ◯ ▻— ◯ ▻— ◯ | |

the rule is

c 99 ▻— 94 ▻— 89 ▻— ◯ ▻— ◯ ▻— ◯ | |

the rule is

d 22 ▻— 31 ▻— 40 ▻— ◯ ▻— ◯ ▻— ◯ | |

the rule is

e 83 ▻— 74 ▻— 65 ▻— ◯ ▻— ◯ ▻— ◯ | |

4 Look at what each machine does to change numbers.
The tables show which numbers come out of each machine.
Write which numbers go into each machine.

a
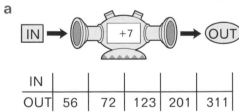

IN					
OUT	56	72	123	201	311

b
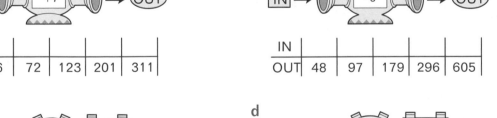

IN					
OUT	48	97	179	296	605

c
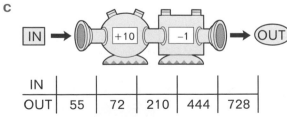

IN					
OUT	55	72	210	444	728

d
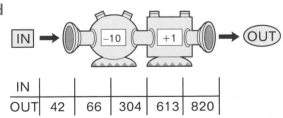

IN					
OUT	42	66	304	613	820

Topic 5: 2D shapes

2D shapes are flat. They can have straight or curved sides.

Shapes with straight sides	
Name	**Sides**
triangle	3
quadrilateral	4
pentagon	5
hexagon	6

Shapes with curved sides

○ circle

○ oval

⌒ semi-circle

Some shapes have right angles

A right angle is a quarter of a whole turn.

Some shapes have several names. ☐ A square and a rectangle ☐ are special types of quadrilateral.

Practice

1 Write the name of each shape.

a _____

b _____

c _____

d _____

e _____

f _____

g _____

h _____

i _____

j _____

k _____

l _____

m _____

n _____

o _____

2 Each of these 2D shapes has sides that go inwards.

Write a name for each shape.

a _____ b _____ c _____

3 Tick all the right angles in each shape.

a   b   c

d   e   f

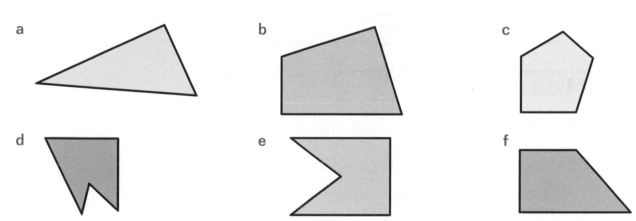

4 Join up these shapes in pairs, where one shape is half of the other.

a   b   c   d

e   f   g   h

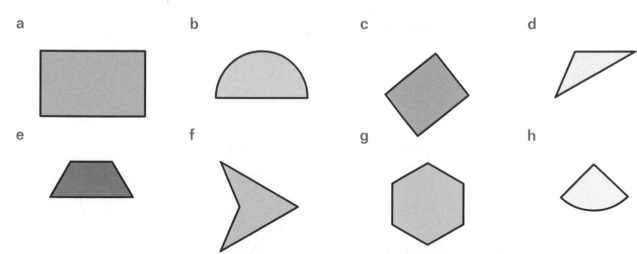

Topic 6: Time

Get started

It takes 5 minutes for the minute hand to move from one number to the next.

60 seconds = 1 minute

60 minutes = 1 hour

24 hours = 1 day

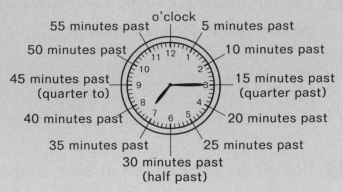

The clock shows 7:15

Practice

1 Write these times in hours and minutes.

a

:

b

:

c

:

d

:

e

:

f

:

g

:

h

:

2 Draw the missing minute hands on the clocks.

a

3:10

b

9:55

c

6:05

d

12:20

Challenge

3 **Answer these problems about time.**

a How many minutes in half an hour? ▢

b How many minutes in quarter of an hour? ▢

c How many minutes in three-quarters of an hour? ▢

d How many hours in a day? ▢

e How many weeks in a year? ▢

f Which month follows August? _____

g Which month comes just before April? _____

h How many days in November? ▢

i How many days in September? ▢

j How many days in a leap year? ▢

4 **How many minutes are there between these two times?**

a   minutes

b    minutes

c   minutes

d   minutes

5 **Write the answers to these problems about time.**

a What time is 30 minutes after 3:15? ▢ : ▢

b What time is 10 minutes after 7:45? ▢ : ▢

c What time is 20 minutes after 3:05? ▢ : ▢

d What time is half an hour after 6:10? ▢ : ▢

e What time is quarter of an hour after 11:25? ▢ : ▢

Topic 1

1 Write the missing number.

$\bigcirc + 8 = 15$

2 Write the answer.

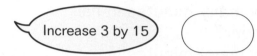
Increase 3 by 15

3 Write in the two missing numbers.

+	1	4	5
2	3	6	
4	5		9
5	6	9	10

4 What number goes into the machine?

IN → +7 → 16

Topic 2

5 Write the missing number.

$\bigcirc - 8 = 12$

6 Write the answer.

Decrease 14 by 6

7 What is the difference?

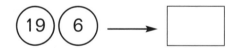
19 6 →

8 What number goes into the machine?

IN → −9 → 6

Topic 3

9 Write 3005 in words.

_____

_____

10 Write these six numbers in order, starting with the smallest.
706, 607, 670, 760, 660, 770

____ ____ ____ ____ ____ ____

11 What is the digit 5 worth?
3512 _____

12 Arrange the three digits to make the smallest possible number.
5, 2, 8 _____

Topic 4

13 Write the answer.

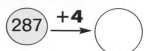

287 **+4** ◯

14 Write the answer.

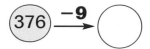

376 **−9** ◯

15 Write the difference between the two numbers.

138 144 ⟶ ◯

16 Write in the missing three numbers.

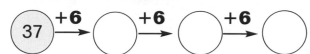

37 **+6** ◯ **+6** ◯ **+6** ◯

Topic 5

17 Name this 2D shape.

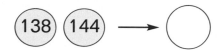

_____

18 Name this 2D shape.

_____

19 Cross the odd one out.

20 Tick all the right angles.

Topic 6

21 Write the time.

◻ : ◻

22 Draw the missing minute hand.

4:25

23 How many days are there in May? ◯

24 How many minutes are there in an hour? ◯

Mark the test. Remember to fill in your score on page 3.

Write your score out of 24. ◻

Add a bonus point if you scored 20 or more.

TOTAL SCORE FOR TEST 1 ◻

Topic 7: Addition

Get started

There are lots of different ways to add two-digit numbers.

Here are two ways:

$$37 \quad + \quad 48$$

$$= \quad 30 + 7 \quad + \quad 40 + 8$$

$$= \quad 30 + 40 \quad + \quad 7 + 8$$

$$= \quad 70 \quad + \quad 15$$

Ans $= \quad 85$

$$\begin{array}{r} 37 \\ + 48 \\ \hline 85 \\ {}_{1} \end{array}$$

Practice

1 Do these additions using your own method.
   Some you will be able to work out in your head.

a 44 + 35 = ☐   b 25 + 32 = ☐   c 62 + 17 = ☐   d 25 + 63 = ☐

e 25 + 35 = ☐   f 45 + 15 = ☐   g 64 + 26 = ☐   h 27 + 53 = ☐

i 37 + 34 = ☐   j 46 + 46 = ☐   k 72 + 19 = ☐   l 47 + 35 = ☐

2 Do these additions. Some you may be able to work out in your head.

a   56   b   75   c   88   d   43   e   76
  + 68   + 46   + 88   + 89   + 57
  ‾‾‾‾   ‾‾‾‾   ‾‾‾‾   ‾‾‾‾   ‾‾‾‾

3 Add the rows across and fill in the yellow boxes. Add the columns down
   and fill in the pink boxes. Add the pink numbers and the yellow numbers –
   they have the same total. Write this total in the blue total boxes.

a
18	24	
16	26	

b
26	34	
14	27	

c
19	26	
37	34	

d
27	36	
18	28	

Challenge

4 Write in the missing digits.

a
```
  3◯
+ 2 3
─────
  5 7
```

b
```
  2 8
+ 3◯
─────
  5 9
```

c
```
  4 3
+◯ 3
─────
  9 6
```

d
```
 ◯5
+ 2 2
─────
  5 7
```

e
```
  4◯
+ 3 3
─────
  7 9
```

f
```
  4◯
+ 3 8
─────
  8 3
```

g
```
  2 6
+ 4◯
─────
  7 2
```

h
```
  5◯
+ 2 6
─────
  8 4
```

i
```
  3 9
+ 2◯
─────
  6 8
```

j
```
  4◯
+ 4 8
─────
  9 5
```

5 Join pairs that total 50.

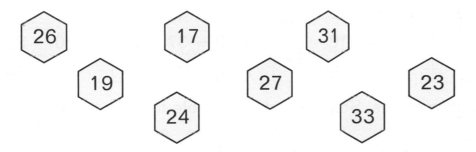

26   17   31

19   27   23

24   33

6 Answer the problems using the five numbers below.

a Write the largest <u>even</u> total you can make by adding two of the numbers. _____

b Write the smallest <u>odd</u> total you can make by adding two of the numbers. _____

c Which three numbers total 90? _____

d Which three numbers total 75? _____

e What is the total of all the numbers? _____

35   16

24   28

38

Topic 8: Subtraction

There are lots of different ways to subtract two-digit numbers.

Here are two ways of solving 53 − 38.

Breaking up 53 into   Counting on from 38 to 53:
40 and 13:   4 13

        5̶3̶
       − 3 8
       _____
         1 5

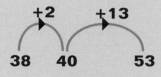

        +2   +13

38   40   53

answer 15

Practice

1 Do these subtractions using your own method.
   Some you will be able to work out in your head.

   a 58 − 24 = ☐   b 75 − 53 = ☐   c 88 − 32 = ☐   d 64 − 34 = ☐

   e 60 − 45 = ☐   f 50 − 18 = ☐   g 70 − 37 = ☐   h 90 − 56 = ☐

   i 62 − 38 = ☐   j 45 − 19 = ☐   k 64 − 27 = ☐   l 72 − 45 = ☐

2 Do these subtractions. Some you may be able to work out in your head.

   a   6 3   b   4 5   c   6 2   d   6 1   e   5 5
     − 2 7   − 1 8   − 3 4   − 2 6   − 2 8
     _____   _____   _____   _____   _____

3 Write the difference between each pair of numbers. Start with the larger
   number in each pair.

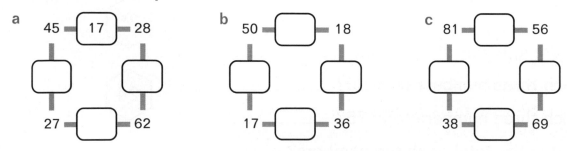

a   45 — 17 — 28

     27 — ☐ — 62

b   50 — ☐ — 18

     17 — ☐ — 36

c   81 — ☐ — 56

     38 — ☐ — 69

4 Write in the missing digits.

a
```
   5◯
 − 4 3
 ─────
   1 4
```

b
```
   6 8
 − 2◯
 ─────
   4 3
```

c
```
  ◯4
 − 4 3
 ─────
   2 1
```

d
```
   9 7
 −◯2
 ─────
   4 5
```

e
```
   8◯
 − 1 8
 ─────
   7 1
```

f
```
   4◯
 − 1 8
 ─────
   2 6
```

g
```
   7 0
 − 3◯
 ─────
   3 6
```

h
```
   5◯
 − 1 8
 ─────
   3 7
```

i
```
   6 2
 − 2◯
 ─────
   3 6
```

j
```
   9◯
 − 4 9
 ─────
   4 4
```

5 Write in the missing numbers in these chains.

a   100 —−19→ ☐ —−19→ ☐ —−19→ ☐ —−19→ ☐

b   100 —−15→ ☐ —−16→ ☐ —−17→ ☐ —−18→ ☐

c   100 —−23→ ☐ —−16→ ☐ —−23→ ☐ —−16→ ☐

6 Answer these problems.

a How much greater is A than B? _____

b What is the difference between F and D? _____

c Which number is 34 less than A? _____

d Which two numbers have a
  difference of 20? _____

e Which two numbers have a
  difference of F? _____

A   91
B   76
C   57
D   48
E   35
F   28

Topic 9: Symmetry

Get started

A line of symmetry is like a mirror line.

One half of the shape is the reflection of the other half.

Lines of symmetry are not always up and down or across the page. They can be sloping.

a mirror line   mirror lines or lines of symmetry

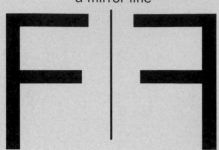   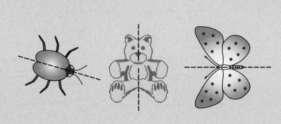

Practice

1 **Draw one line of symmetry on each shape.**

a    b   c   d

e   f   g   h

2 **Tick the square that is a reflection of pattern A.**

a mirror line

A   B   C   D   E

3 Draw the reflection of each shape.

Colour the completed picture.

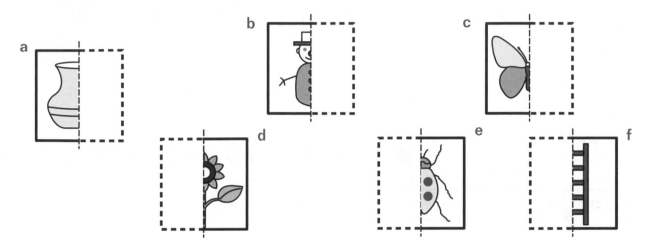

4 Complete each sticker

What is the mystery letter on each sticker?

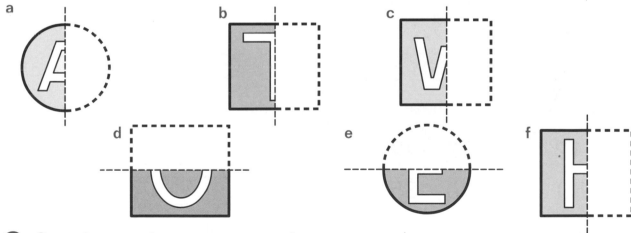

5 Complete each symmetry word.

Make up more words of your own.

Topic 10: Sequences and patterns

Get started

Sequences follow on in order. They often make repeating patterns.

Shape sequence   **Number sequence**   **Line sequence**

□ □ ○ □ □ ○ □ □   1 2 2 1 2 2 1 2 2   / ⌐ \ / ⌐ \ / ⌐ \

Some number sequences go up or down in the same size steps.

Sequence of odd numbers   **Sequence of even numbers**   **Multiples of 5**

31, 33, 35, 37, 39, 41 …   96, 98, 100, 102, 104 …   5, 10, 15, 20, 25, 30, 35 …

Practice

1 Continue each of these sequences.

a △ ▯ ▯ ▯ △ ▯ ▯ ▯ _ _ _   b ○ □ ▽ ○ □ ▽ _ _ _

c 7 7 4 7 7 4 _ _ _   d 1 2 3 3 2 1 _ _ _

e | ○ ⊘ | ○ ⊘ _ _ _   f ⊂=⊃ ⊂=⊃ _ _ _

2 Continue each of these number sequences.

a 12 22 32 42 52 62 ☐ ☐ ☐

b 50 45 40 35 30 25 ☐ ☐ ☐

c 21 23 25 27 29 31 ☐ ☐ ☐

d 80 78 76 74 72 70 ☐ ☐ ☐

e 18 22 26 30 34 38 ☐ ☐ ☐

Challenge

3 Write the numbers in order in the tables. Start with the smallest.

a	odd numbers		141 123 107 130
	not odd numbers		159 174 168 142
b	multiples of 5		25 40 60 95
	not multiples of 5		35 74 38 52
c	multiples of 2		31 50 45 37
	not multiples of 2		28 17 58 62
d	multiples of 10		10 45 90 60
	not multiples of 10		80 15 50 100

4 Write the missing numbers in these sequences.

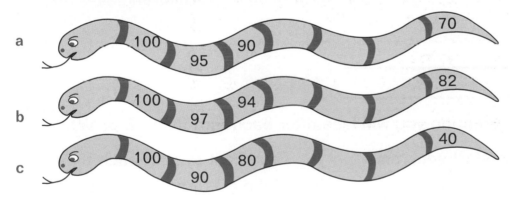

a 100 95 90 70

b 100 97 94 82

c 100 90 80 40

5 Write the numbers that follow on from each of these.

a next odd number

299 ➡

b next even number

598 ➡

c next multiple of 5

75 ➡

d next multiple of 10

120 ➡

e next multiple of 2

34 ➡

f next multiple of 3

33 ➡

Topic 11: Position, direction and angles

Get started

  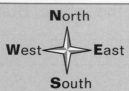 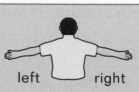

turning clockwise   turning anticlockwise   four compass points   You have a right side and a left side.

quarter turn   half turn   three-quarters turn   complete turn

1 right angle $= \frac{1}{4}$ turn   2 right angles $= \frac{1}{2}$ turn   3 right angles $= \frac{3}{4}$ turn   4 right angles $= 1$ turn

Practice

1 Write which direction you will face after each turn (N, S, E or W).

Face North to start each time

a Make a $\frac{1}{4}$ turn clockwise. _____

b Make a $\frac{1}{2}$ turn anticlockwise. _____

c Make a $\frac{3}{4}$ turn clockwise. _____

Face East to start each time

d Make a $\frac{1}{2}$ turn clockwise. _____

e Make a $\frac{1}{4}$ turn anticlockwise. _____

f Make a $\frac{3}{4}$ turn clockwise. _____

Face West to start each time

g Make a $\frac{3}{4}$ turn clockwise. _____

h Make a $\frac{1}{4}$ turn anticlockwise. _____

i Make a $\frac{3}{4}$ turn anticlockwise. _____

Face South to start each time

j Make a $\frac{1}{4}$ turn anticlockwise. _____

k Make a $\frac{1}{2}$ turn clockwise. _____

l Make a $\frac{3}{4}$ turn clockwise. _____

Challenge

2 Tick the right angle in each set.

a

b

c

d

e

f

3 Start from North each time. Write what you will see after the turn.

a Turn to the East

_____

b Turn to the West

_____

c Turn to the South

_____

d $\frac{3}{4}$ turn clockwise

_____

e $\frac{3}{4}$ turn anticlockwise

_____

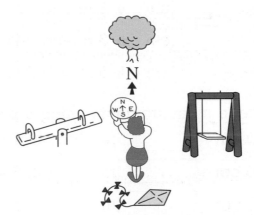

4 Start from the red square each time.

a Go 1 square N then 2 squares E.
Write P in the box.

b Go 1 square W then 2 squares N.
Write Q in the box.

c Go 2 squares E then 2 squares S.
Write R in the box.

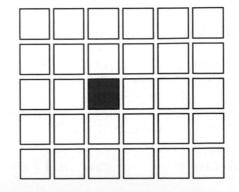

Topic 12: Length

There are **100 centimetres** in **1 metre**.

100 centimetres = 1 metre   100 cm = 1 m

625 cm = 6 metres and 25 centimetres

625 cm = 6.25 m

The point separates the metres from the centimetres

Practice

1 Write how many centimetres are in each of these measurements.

a 2 metres = ☐ cm   b 1 m and 20 cm = ☐ cm   c 2.45 m = ☐ cm

d 5 metres = ☐ cm   e 1 m and 77 cm = ☐ cm   f 3.05 m = ☐ cm

g $\frac{1}{2}$ metre = ☐ cm   h 3 m and 4 cm = ☐ cm   i 5.50 m = ☐ cm

j $3\frac{1}{2}$ metre = ☐ cm   k 5 m and 29 cm = ☐ cm   l 8.32 m = ☐ cm

2 Write these measurements using a point like this: 3.50 m

a 4 m + 70 cm = ☐ m   b 1 m + 25 cm = ☐ m

c 3 m + 70 cm = ☐ m   d 6 m + 15 cm = ☐ m

e 8 m + 35 cm = ☐ m   f 3 m − 20 cm = ☐ m

g 2 m − 90 cm = ☐ m   h 5 m − 10 cm = ☐ m

i 8 m − 50 cm = ☐ m   j 9 m − 5 cm = ☐ m

3 What must be added to each measurement to make 1 metre?

a 35 cm + ☐ cm   b 55 cm + ☐ cm   c 85 cm + ☐ cm

d 15 cm + ☐ cm   e 64 cm + ☐ cm   f 32 cm + ☐ cm

g 96 cm + ☐ cm   h 17 cm + ☐ cm

Challenge

4 Work out the answers to these problems.
Write each answer using a point like this: 3.2 m

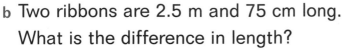

a A 3 metre length of ribbon has 25 cm cut off.
What length remains?

b Two ribbons are 2.5 m and 75 cm long.
What is the difference in length?

c One ribbon is twice as long as the other.
The short ribbon is 80 cm.
What is the length of the long ribbon?

d A ribbon measuring 3 metres is cut in half.
How long is each piece?

e Two ribbons are 50 cm and 80 cm long.
What is their total length?

5 Write each measurement to the nearest centimetre.

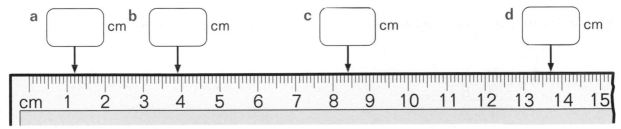

a ___ cm b ___ cm c ___ cm d ___ cm

6 Write each measurement to the nearest half centimetre. The first one is an example.

example $1\frac{1}{2}$ cm a ___ cm b ___ cm c ___ cm d ___ cm

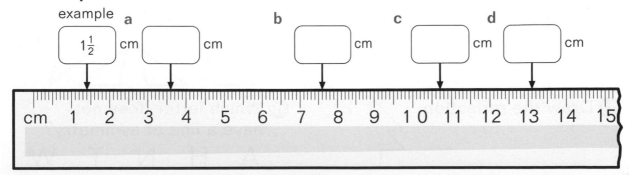

Test 2 (Score 1 mark for every correct answer.)

Topic 7

1 What is the total of 38 and 49?

2 Calculate the answer.
$$\begin{array}{r} 6\,7 \\ +\,5\,5 \\ \hline \end{array}$$

3 Write in the missing digit.

$$\begin{array}{r} 4\,\bigcirc \\ +\,3\ \ 5 \\ \hline 8\ \ 0 \end{array}$$

4 Write in the missing number.

15	35	50
25	$\bigcirc$	80
40	90	130

Topic 8

5 What is the difference between 74 and 32?

6 Calculate the answer.
$$\begin{array}{r} 7\,2 \\ -\,4\,6 \\ \hline \end{array}$$

7 Write in the missing digit.

$$\begin{array}{r} 5\,\bigcirc \\ -\,3\ \ 8 \\ \hline 1\ \ 4 \end{array}$$

8 Decrease 85 by 58.

Topic 9

9 Draw one line of symmetry on the shape.

10 Tick the reflection of the first shape.

11 Draw the reflection.

12 Which letter does not have a line of symmetry?

A H N T W

Topic 10

⑬ Write the next number.

4 8 12 16 20 24 ▢

⑭ Write the missing number.

35 40 ▢ **50 55 60**

⑮ Which number is not odd?

| 135 | 449 | 823 | 227 |
| 271 | | 732 | |

⑯ Write in the next even number.

298 ⟶ ⬭

Topic 11

⑰ Face South then make a $\frac{1}{4}$ turn clockwise. In which direction are you facing?

_____

⑱ Tick the right angle.

⑲ Tick all the right hands.

⑳ The letter N is turned clockwise through 1 right angle. Draw what it will look like after the turn.

| N | |

Topic 12

㉑ Write in centimetres.

$2\frac{1}{2}$ metres = ▢ **cm**

㉒ Write in centimetres.

3.75 m = ▢ **cm**

㉓ What is left when you cut 45 cm from 1 metre? ▢ **cm**

㉔ What is the total of 70 cm and 50 cm? ▢ **. m**

Mark the test. Remember to fill in your score on page 3.

Write your score out of 24. ▢

Add a bonus point if you scored 20 or more.

TOTAL SCORE FOR TEST 2 ▢

Topic 13: Addition and subtraction

Addition undoes subtraction

$72 - 39 = \boxed{33}$
To undo the subtraction, add 39

$\boxed{33} + 39 = 72$ ... which is what you started with.

Subtraction undoes addition

$34 + 57 = \boxed{91}$
To undo the addition, subtract 57

$\boxed{91} - 57 = 34$ ... which is what you started with.

You can use these facts to check that you have subtracted correctly:

```
  5 2  check    1 4
- 3 8          + 3 8
-----          -----
  1 4            5 2
```

Practice

1 Write and check your answers.
You may be able to work some out in your head.

a
```
  3 6
+ 3 8
-----
```

b
```
  5 4
- 2 6
-----
```

c
```
  4 5
+ 1 5
-----
```

d
```
  7 1
- 2 6
-----
```

e
```
  6 7
+ 2 4
-----
```

f
```
  6 0
- 4 9
-----
```

g
```
  4 6
+ 4 6
-----
```

h
```
  5 2
- 2 6
-----
```

i
```
  2 7
+ 5 7
-----
```

j
```
  9 3
- 4 8
-----
```

2 Work out the answers. For each question go from left to right.

a $28 + 34 - 18 = \boxed{}$

b $71 - 45 + 28 = \boxed{}$

c $80 - 34 - 15 = \boxed{}$

d $29 + 29 + 29 = \boxed{}$

e $35 + 24 + 26 = \boxed{}$

f $94 - 67 - 15 = \boxed{}$

g $80 - 16 - 49 = \boxed{}$

h $75 - 28 + 28 = \boxed{}$

Challenge

3 Write the missing numbers in these chains.

a 58 $\xrightarrow{+25}$ ☐ $\xrightarrow{-37}$ ☐ $\xrightarrow{+28}$ ☐

b 94 $\xrightarrow{-28}$ ☐ $\xrightarrow{+15}$ ☐ $\xrightarrow{-27}$ ☐

c 42 $\xrightarrow{+48}$ ☐ $\xrightarrow{-37}$ ☐ $\xrightarrow{-35}$ ☐

d 83 $\xrightarrow{-36}$ ☐ $\xrightarrow{-17}$ ☐ $\xrightarrow{-25}$ ☐

e 100 $\xrightarrow{-78}$ ☐ $\xrightarrow{+38}$ ☐ $\xrightarrow{+29}$ ☐

4 Write in the missing digits.

a
```
  2 6
+ 5◯
─────
  8 3
```

b
```
  7 4
- 2◯
─────
  4 6
```

c
```
  5◯
+ 3 9
─────
  9 1
```

d
```
  5◯
- 3 6
─────
  1 4
```

e
```
  3 6
+◯4
─────
  9 0
```

f
```
  ◯3
- 3 9
─────
  2 4
```

g
```
  ◯6
+ 5 4
─────
  1 0 0
```

h
```
  7 3
-◯6
─────
  5 7
```

i
```
  5 7
+◯6
─────
  9 3
```

j
```
  1 0 0
-◯◯
─────
    5 6
```

5 Answer these problems, using the numbers in yellow.

a What is the total of the first three numbers? _____

b What is the difference between the first
   and last numbers? _____

c Which two numbers have a total
   of 91? _____

d Which two numbers have a difference of 55? _____

e Which two numbers total 75? _____

 55 17 81 36 72 39

Topic 14: Multiplication

Get started

x	0	1	2	3	4	5	6	7	8	9	10
2	0	2	4	6	8	10	12	14	16	18	20
3	0	3	6	9	12	15	18	21	24	27	30
4	0	4	8	12	16	20	24	28	32	36	40
5	0	5	10	15	20	25	30	35	40	45	50
10	0	10	20	30	40	50	60	70	80	90	100

You can multiply in any order:

4×6 has the same answer as 6×4

You should know the multiplication facts shown in the table by heart.

Can you see that the answers to 10× are double the answers to 5×?

Practice

1 Answer each block of table facts as quickly as you can.

a $2 \times \ 2 =$ __ b $5 \times \ 5 =$ __ c $10 \times \ 5 =$ __ d $3 \times \ 5 =$ __ e $4 \times \ 5 =$ __

$2 \times \ 3 =$ __ $5 \times \ 2 =$ __ $10 \times \ 2 =$ __ $3 \times \ 2 =$ __ $4 \times \ 2 =$ __

$2 \times \ 7 =$ __ $5 \times \ 7 =$ __ $10 \times \ 7 =$ __ $3 \times \ 7 =$ __ $4 \times \ 7 =$ __

$2 \times 10 =$ __ $5 \times 10 =$ __ $10 \times 10 =$ __ $3 \times 10 =$ __ $4 \times 10 =$ __

$2 \times \ 8 =$ __ $5 \times \ 8 =$ __ $10 \times \ 8 =$ __ $3 \times \ 8 =$ __ $4 \times \ 8 =$ __

$9 \times \ 2 =$ __ $9 \times \ 5 =$ __ $9 \times 10 =$ __ $9 \times \ 3 =$ __ $9 \times \ 4 =$ __

$6 \times \ 2 =$ __ $6 \times \ 5 =$ __ $6 \times 10 =$ __ $6 \times \ 3 =$ __ $6 \times \ 4 =$ __

$4 \times \ 2 =$ __ $4 \times \ 5 =$ __ $4 \times 10 =$ __ $4 \times \ 3 =$ __ $4 \times \ 4 =$ __

$5 \times \ 2 =$ __ $3 \times \ 2 =$ __ $3 \times 10 =$ __ $3 \times \ 3 =$ __ $3 \times \ 4 =$ __

$0 \times \ 2 =$ __ $0 \times \ 5 =$ __ $0 \times 10 =$ __ $0 \times \ 3 =$ __ $0 \times \ 4 =$ __

2 Complete these grids.

a

×	4	7	9
2			
5			
10			

b

×	3	6	8
2			
5			
10			

c

×	4	7	8
3			
4			
5			

Challenge

3 Complete each table.

a
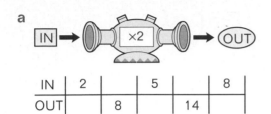

IN	2		5		8	
OUT		8		14		

b
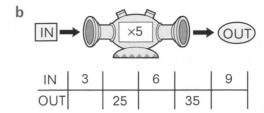

IN	3		6		9	
OUT		25		35		

c
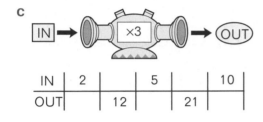

IN	2		5		10	
OUT		12		21		

d
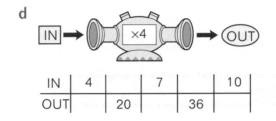

IN	4		7		10	
OUT		20		36		

4 Write four different facts for each number.

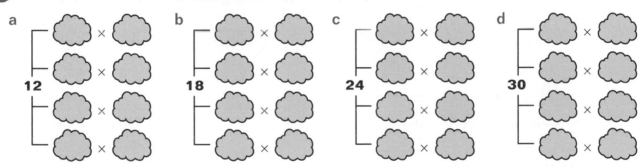

5 These numbers are answers to multiplication by 2, 3, 4 or 5.
Write one multiplication fact for each answer.

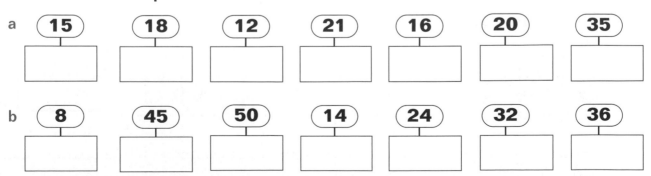

Get started

A prism is a 3D shape with matching ends.

Slices of a prism are always the same size and shape all the way through.

triangular prism

pentagonal prism

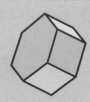
hexagonal prism

Cubes and cuboids are special types of prism.

The shape of the ends gives the prism its name.

Practice

1 **Name each of these 3D shapes.**
   For prisms, use the full name, such as 'triangular prism'.

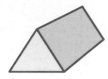

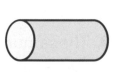

a _____   b _____   c _____   d _____
_____

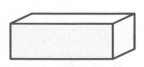

e _____   f _____   g _____   h _____

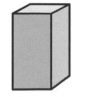

i _____   j _____   k _____   l _____
_____

Challenge

2 Tick the odd one out in each set. Write why it is the odd one out.

a
 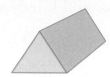 

_____

b

_____

c

_____

d

_____

3 Write ALWAYS, SOMETIMES or NEVER.

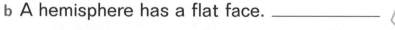
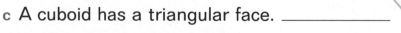
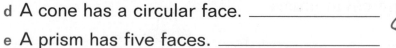

a A prism has a square or
rectangular face. _____

b A hemisphere has a flat face. _____

c A cuboid has a triangular face. _____

d A cone has a circular face. _____

e A prism has five faces. _____

Topic 16: Weight and mass

Get started

Mass and weight are not quite the same.

Mass is the amount of matter or material in an object. An elephant has more mass than a mouse.

Weight is the measurement of the force of gravity on an object.

Many books use the word 'weight' to mean the same as 'mass'.

Metric units of mass are **grams** and **kilograms**.

There are 1000 grams in 1 kilogram.

$$1000 \text{ g} = 1 \text{ kg}$$

$$500 \text{ g} = \tfrac{1}{2} \text{ kg}$$

kilo at the start of a word means 1000.

Practice

1 Write how many grams are in each of these masses.

a 2 kg = [   ] g   b 5 kg = [   ] g   c 3 kg = [   ] g

d 6 kg = [   ] g   e $\tfrac{1}{2}$ kg = [   ] g   f $1\tfrac{1}{2}$ kg = [   ] g

2 Write the answers.

a How many 500 g will balance 1 kg? [   ]

b How many 200 g will balance 1 kg? [   ]

c How many 100 g will balance 1 kg? [   ]

d How many 50 g will balance 1 kg? [   ]

e How many 100 g will balance $\tfrac{1}{2}$ kg? [   ]

f How many 50 g will balance $\tfrac{1}{2}$ kg? [   ]

500 g   200 g   100 g   50 g

3 Write the mass of each parcel in grams.

a

[   ] g →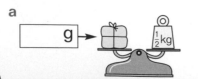

b

[   ] g →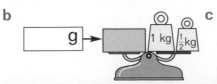

c

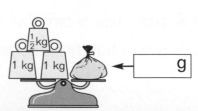 ← [   ] g

Challenge

4 **Answer these problems.**

a What is the difference in weight between the parcels? [ ] g

b What is the total weight of the parcels? [ ] g

c How much heavier is one parcel than the other? [ ] g

d How heavy are both these parcels altogether? [ ] g

e How much lighter is one parcel than the other? [ ] g

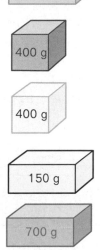

200 g   500 g

300 g   400 g

600 g   400 g

150 g   150 g

1 kg   700 g

5 **Write each weight to the nearest half kilogram.**

a   b   c   d

[ ] kg   [ ] kg   [ ] kg   [ ] kg

Topic 17: Charts and diagrams

Information is sometimes shown using Venn diagrams and Carroll diagrams.

Here is the same information shown on both kinds of diagram:

Venn diagram

Children's shoes

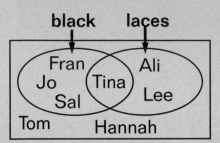

Carroll diagram

Children's shoes

	black	not black	
laces	Tina	Ali Lee	
not laces	Fran Jo Sal	Tom Hannah	

Each part of the diagram gives you different information.

You can see that: Tina has black shoes with laces.

Tom's and Hannah's shoes are not black and do not have laces.

Practice

1 Write the numbers from the Venn diagram on the Carroll diagram.

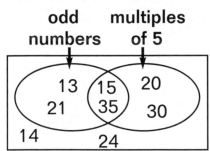

	odd numbers	not odd numbers
multiples of 5		
not multiples of 5		

2 Write the initials from the Carroll diagram on the Venn diagram.

	has brothers	no brothers
has sisters	**R**ex **T**oni	**J**ames **M**ina
no sisters	**G**eorge **H**armit	**S**cott **F**leur

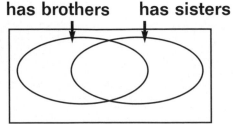

Challenge

3 Complete these diagrams.

a Write the numbers on the Venn diagram.

6, 11, 5, 12, 18, 8, 15, 3

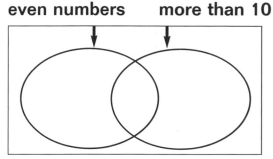

b Write the fruit names on the Carroll diagram.

apple, orange, cherry, peach, plum, banana, lemon

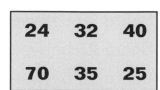

4 Write these six numbers on this type of Venn diagram.

24	32	40
70	35	25

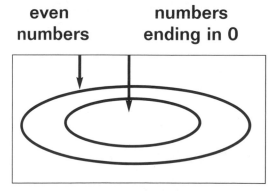

Why do you think one loop is inside the other?

_____

Topic 18: Division

Get started

The **sign for division** is ÷
Division can mean two things:

- sharing things equally

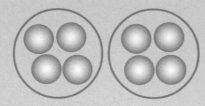

sharing 8 equally between
2 makes 4 each

8 ÷ 2 = 4

- grouping into sets of the same size

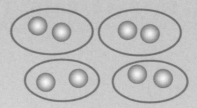

sharing 8 into twos makes 4 sets

8 ÷ 2 = 4

Practice

1 **Write the answers.**

a How many twos in 12? ☐   b How many twos in 20? ☐

c How many twos in 16? ☐   d How many fives in 20? ☐

e How many fives in 35? ☐   f How many fives in 45? ☐

g How many tens in 30? ☐   h How many tens in 80? ☐

i How many tens in 70? ☐   j How many twos in 14? ☐

2 **Write the answers.**

a Share 14 between 2 ☐   b Share 20 between 2 ☐

c Share 12 between 2 ☐   d Share 25 between 5 ☐

e Share 40 between 5 ☐   f Share 15 between 5 ☐

g Share 20 between 10 ☐   h Share 50 between 10 ☐

i Share 90 between 10 ☐   j Share 16 between 2 ☐

3 **Answer these as quickly as you can.**

a $14 \div 2 =$ ☐   b $15 \div 5 =$ ☐   c $40 \div 10 =$ ☐   d $30 \div 5 =$ ☐

e $18 \div 2 =$ ☐   f $45 \div 5 =$ ☐   g $12 \div 2 =$ ☐   h $16 \div 2 =$ ☐

Challenge

4 **Halve each number and write the answer.**

a (16) ⟶ ◯ b (18) ⟶ ◯ c (12) ⟶ ◯ d (14) ⟶ ◯

e (40) ⟶ ◯ f (60) ⟶ ◯ g (80) ⟶ ◯ h (20) ⟶ ◯

i (30) ⟶ ◯ j (50) ⟶ ◯ k (70) ⟶ ◯ l (90) ⟶ ◯

5 **Complete each table.**

a
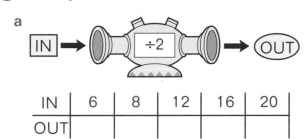

IN	6	8	12	16	20
OUT					

b
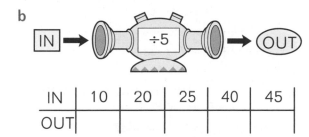

IN	10	20	25	40	45
OUT					

c
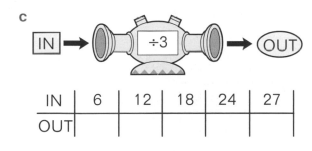

IN	6	12	18	24	27
OUT					

d
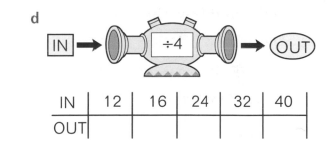

IN	12	16	24	32	40
OUT					

6 **Write the answers.**

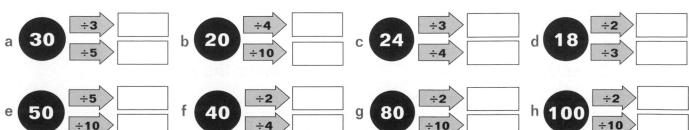

a **30** ÷3 ☐ ÷5 ☐

b **20** ÷4 ☐ ÷10 ☐

c **24** ÷3 ☐ ÷4 ☐

d **18** ÷2 ☐ ÷3 ☐

e **50** ÷5 ☐ ÷10 ☐

f **40** ÷2 ☐ ÷4 ☐

g **80** ÷2 ☐ ÷10 ☐

h **100** ÷2 ☐ ÷10 ☐

Test 3 (Score 1 mark for every correct answer.)

1 Join each number sentence to its answer.

⟨ 88 − 39 ⟩   ⟨ 47 ⟩
⟨ 19 + 29 ⟩   ⟨ 48 ⟩
⟨ 65 − 18 ⟩   ⟨ 49 ⟩

2 Write in the missing digits.

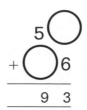

$$5\bigcirc$$
$$+\ \bigcirc 6$$
$$\overline{9\ \ 3}$$

3 Write the answer.

46 + 54 − 27 = ☐

4 Write in the missing number.

Topic 14

5 Write in the missing number.

8 × ☐ = 40

6 Write in the missing number.

☐ × 4 = 24

7 How much is the pile of 2p coins worth?

☐

8 Complete the multiplication grid.

×	4	5	7
2	8	10	
3		15	
5	20		35

Topic 15

9 Name the shape.

_____

10 Name the shape.

_____

11 Name the shape.

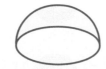

_____

12 Name the shape.

_____

Topic 16

13 How many $\frac{1}{2}$ kg weights balance 2 kg?

14 500 g + 700 g =

[ ] kg and [ ] g

15 What is the reading on the scales?

[ ]

16 What is the reading on the scales?

[ ]

Topic 17

17 Draw this card on the Venn diagram.

spots

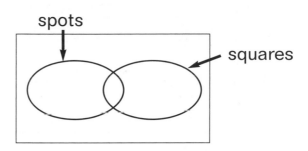

squares

18 Now draw it on the Carroll diagram.

19 Draw this card on the Venn diagram.

spots	no spots	
		square
		not square

20 Now draw it on the Carroll diagram.

Topic 18

21 Write the answer. **35 ÷ 5 =** [ ]

22 Write the missing number. ◯ ÷2=9

23 Write the answer. ⇨ [ ]

24 Halve the number.  ◯

Mark the test. Remember to fill in your score on page 3.

Write your score out of 24. [ ]

Add a bonus point if you scored 20 or more.

TOTAL SCORE FOR TEST 3 [ ]

Topic 19: Tens and hundreds

Get started

Multiplying by ten

When you multiply by 10, the digits move one place left and a zero fills the gap.

$4\,7 \times 10 = 470 \quad 7\,0 \times 10 = 700$

470   700

Dividing by ten

When you divide by 10, the digits move one place right and a zero can be lost.

$3\,6\,0 \div 10 = 3\,6 \quad 5\,0\,0 \div 10 = 50$

36   50

Rounding to the nearest ten or hundred

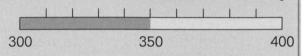

70   75   85

Round up to the next ten if the number is half-way or more.

Round down if it is less than half-way.

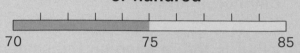

300   350   400

Round up to the next hundred if the number is half-way or more.

Round down if it is less than half-way.

The symbol $\approx$ means approximately or nearly.

Practice

1 Write the answers. Work them out in your head.

Multiply these numbers by 10

Divide these numbers by 10

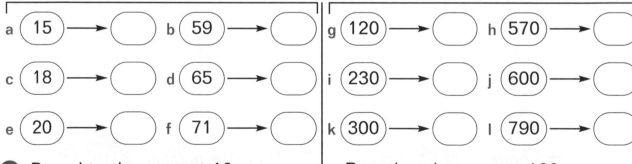

a (15) ⟶ ( )   b (59) ⟶ ( )   g (120) ⟶ ( )   h (570) ⟶ ( )

c (18) ⟶ ( )   d (65) ⟶ ( )   i (230) ⟶ ( )   j (600) ⟶ ( )

e (20) ⟶ ( )   f (71) ⟶ ( )   k (300) ⟶ ( )   l (790) ⟶ ( )

2 Round to the nearest 10

Round to the nearest 100

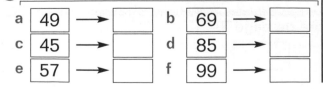
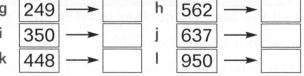

a	49 →	b	69 →	g	249 →	h	562 →
c	45 →	d	85 →	i	350 →	j	637 →
e	57 →	f	99 →	k	448 →	l	950 →

Challenge

3 Write the answers.

a Join each number to its nearest 10.

(35)   (43)   (56)   (75)   (84)

| 0   10   20   30   40   50   60   70   80   90   100 |

(22)   (31)   (47)   (68)   (95)

b Join each number to its nearest 100.

(275)   (422)   (551)   (693)   (762)

| 0   100   200   300   400   500   600   700   800   900   1000 |

(350)   (505)   (639)   (747)   (949)

4 Complete each table.

a
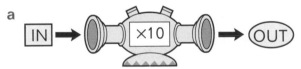

IN	11		22		60
OUT		160		350	

b

IN → ÷10 → OUT

IN	40		370		750
OUT		12		42	

5 Join each number to its nearest 10.

< 345 >   < 472 >   < 454 >   < 538 >   < 591 >

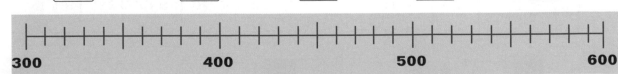

300   400   500   600

Topic 20: Fractions and shapes

Get started

The bottom number in a fraction tells you how many equal parts there are.

The top number tells you how many of those parts you are dealing with.

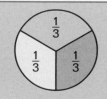

thirds

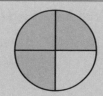

$\frac{3}{4}$ is shaded and $\frac{1}{4}$ is not

The same fraction can look different.

All these are the same as a half.

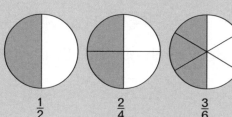

$\frac{1}{2}$ $\frac{2}{4}$ $\frac{3}{6}$

Practice

1 Write the fraction of each shape that is shaded.

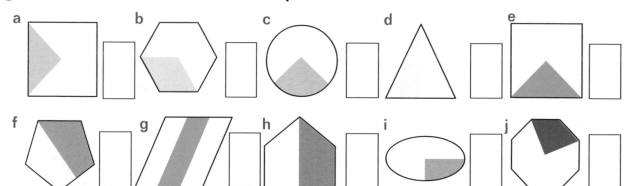

2 Write the fraction of each shape that is shaded.

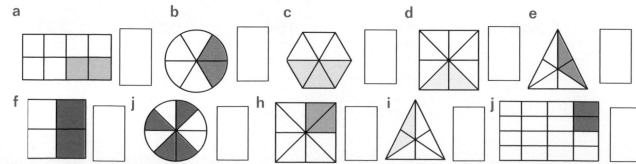

Challenge

3 What fraction is shaded? Write each fraction in two ways.

a 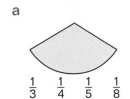   b 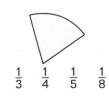   c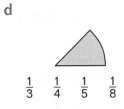

d 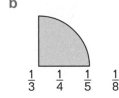   e 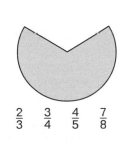   f

4 What fraction of the whole circle can you see? Circle the correct answer.

a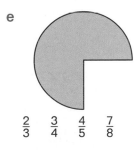

$\frac{1}{3}$ $\frac{1}{4}$ $\frac{1}{5}$ $\frac{1}{8}$

b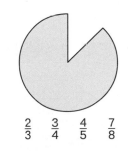

$\frac{1}{3}$ $\frac{1}{4}$ $\frac{1}{5}$ $\frac{1}{8}$

c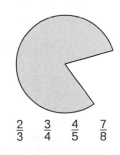

$\frac{1}{3}$ $\frac{1}{4}$ $\frac{1}{5}$ $\frac{1}{8}$

d

$\frac{1}{3}$ $\frac{1}{4}$ $\frac{1}{5}$ $\frac{1}{8}$

e

$\frac{2}{3}$ $\frac{3}{4}$ $\frac{4}{5}$ $\frac{7}{8}$

f

$\frac{2}{3}$ $\frac{3}{4}$ $\frac{4}{5}$ $\frac{7}{8}$

g

$\frac{2}{3}$ $\frac{3}{4}$ $\frac{4}{5}$ $\frac{7}{8}$

h

$\frac{2}{3}$ $\frac{3}{4}$ $\frac{4}{5}$ $\frac{7}{8}$

5 Write the fraction of each pie that has been eaten.

a   b   c   d   e

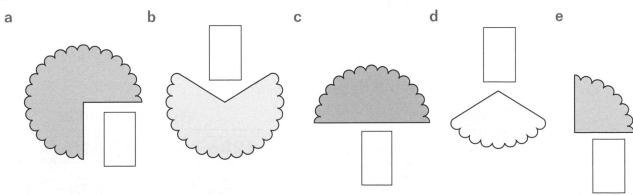

Get started

There are eight coins from 1p to £2

We write money using a decimal point.

100p = £1.00

decimal point

Money can also be notes.

£5 = £5.00
£2.75 = 275p
£1.05 = 105p
120p = £1.20
96p = £0.96

Practice

1 Write the change you would receive from the coin shown at the top.

a (10p)   b (20p)   c (50p)   d (£1)

a:
7p [ ] p
3p [ ] p
5p [ ] p
2p [ ] p

b:
10p [ ] p
15p [ ] p
11p [ ] p
17p [ ] p

c:
10p [ ] p
20p [ ] p
5p [ ] p
2p [ ] p

d:
20p [ ] p
50p [ ] p
10p [ ] p
5p [ ] p

2 Write these amounts in a different way.

Write as pennies		Write as pounds	
a £1.45 [ ] p	b £4.01 [ ] p	g 120p £ [ ]	h 518p £ [ ]
c £2.05 [ ] p	d £6.18 [ ] p	i 225p £ [ ]	j 672p £ [ ]
e £3.95 [ ] p	f £8.79 [ ] p	k 305p £ [ ]	l 934p £ [ ]

Challenge

3 Write these totals. Use the decimal point like this: £2.25

a (£1) £ [___]
   50p

b (£2) £ [___]
   £1.50

c (80p) £ [___]
   70p

d (£1.50) £ [___]
   £1.20

e (£1) £ [___]
   75p

f (£1) £ [___]
   £2.25

g (50p) £ [___]
   90p

h (£1.30) £ [___]
   £1.40

i (£1) £ [___]
   5p

j (£5) £ [___]
   £2.50

k (80p) £ [___]
   40p

l (£1.50) £ [___]
   £1.50

4 Answer these problems.

a I buy two tickets that cost 75p each.
  How much change will I get from £5? [___]

b I share £5 evenly with my sister.
  How much will we each have? [___]

c I have £5 and spend £4.25.
  How much money will I have left? [___]

d I buy cans of lemonade that cost 55p each.
  How many cans can I buy with £5? [___]

e I received £3.25 change from £5.
  How much did I spend? [___]

5 Which <u>two</u> coins from the purse would you offer for each total?

a 70p   60p   choose → [___] and [___]

b £1.50 £1.20 choose → [___] and [___]

c £1.50 54p   choose → [___] and [___]

d 35p   25p   choose → [___] and [___]

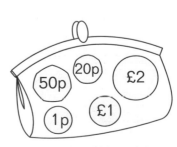

Topic 22: Capacity

Get started

Capacity is about how much something holds.

Metric units of capacity are litres and millilitres.

ml is short for millilitre
l is short for litre

There are **1000 millilitres** in **1 litre**.

$$1000 \text{ ml} = 1 \text{ l}$$
$$500 \text{ ml} = \tfrac{1}{2} \text{ l}$$

milli at the start of a word means thousandths.

Be careful – the **l** can look like the number 1!

Practice

1 Write how many millilitres are in each of these capacities.

a 2 l = ☐ ml   b 5 l = ☐ ml   c 3 l = ☐ ml   d 6 l = ☐ ml

e $\frac{1}{2}$ l = ☐ ml   f $1\frac{1}{2}$ l = ☐ ml   g $3\frac{1}{2}$ l = ☐ ml   h $2\frac{1}{2}$ l = ☐ ml

2 Write the answers.

a How many 500 ml containers will fill a 1 litre jug? ☐

b How many 250 ml containers will fill a 1 litre jug? ☐

c How many 100 ml containers will fill a 1 litre jug? ☐

d How many 50 ml containers will fill a 1 litre jug? ☐

e How many 5 ml spoons will fill a 100 ml bottle? ☐

3 Write how many ml are in each measuring jug.

a  ☐ ml

b ☐ ml

c 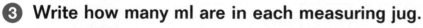 ☐ ml

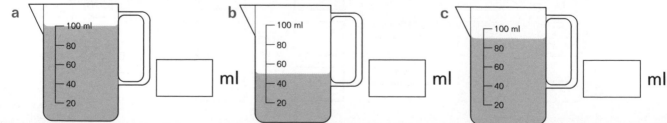

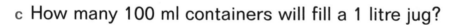

Challenge

4 Answer these problems.

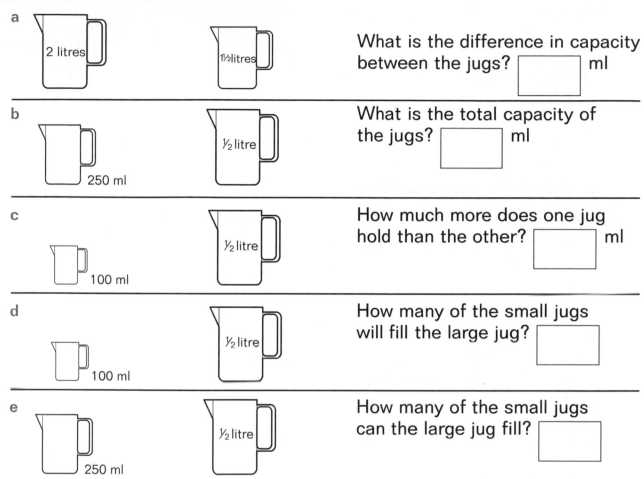

a   2 litres   1½litres   What is the difference in capacity between the jugs? ☐ ml

b   250 ml   ½ litre   What is the total capacity of the jugs? ☐ ml

c   100 ml   ½ litre   How much more does one jug hold than the other? ☐ ml

d   100 ml   ½ litre   How many of the small jugs will fill the large jug? ☐

e   250 ml   ½ litre   How many of the small jugs can the large jug fill? ☐

5 Write each reading to the nearest litre.

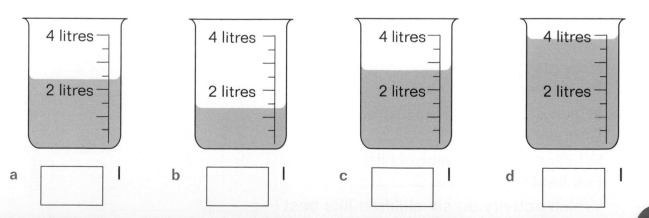

a ☐ l   b ☐ l   c ☐ l   d ☐ l

Topic 23: Graphs

Some graphs have pictures.	Some graphs have bars or columns.
Each picture stands for a number.	You must look carefully at the numbered axis to see what <u>scale</u> is being used.
Look for the <u>key</u> to see how many each picture stands for.	The scale does not always go up in ones.

Practice

1 **Read the key and answer these questions about bedtimes.**

a How many children go to bed at nine o'clock? _____

b How many children go to bed at seven o'clock? _____

c How many children go to bed at half-past eight? _____

d At which time do ten children go to bed? _____

e At which time do nine children go to bed? _____

Bedtimes

Key

= 2 children

7:00

7:30

8:00

8:30

9:00

2 **Read the scale and answer these questions about favourite activities.**

a How many children like playing on a computer best? _____

b How many children like reading best? _____

c How many children like making things best? _____

d Which activity do five children like best? _____

e Which activity do eight children like best? _____

f Which activity do six children like best? _____

Favourite activity

number of children

10
8
6
4
2
0

computer swimming football reading making things

Challenge

3 Answer these questions about the bar graph.

a What has a life span of about
15 years? _____

b How much longer than a horse is a
human expected to live? _____

c What is expected to live 50 years
longer than a trout? _____

d Which should live longer than 50 years?
_____

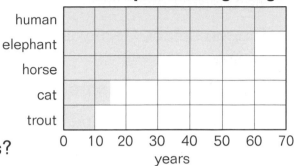

Life span of living things

4 Answer these questions about the bar graph.

a What is the least favourite drink?

_____

b What is the favourite drink? _____

c How many people do not have a
favourite drink? _____

d How many more people like
squash than water? _____

e How many more people like milk than coffee? _____

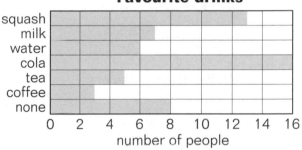

Favourite drinks

5 Answer these questions about the column graph.

a How much was collected on
Thursday?

b How much was collected
on Monday?

c How much was collected
on Tuesday?

d How much was collected
on Wednesday?

e How much more was collected
on Friday than on Thursday?

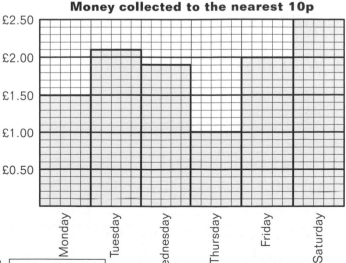

Money collected to the nearest 10p

Topic 24: Fractions and numbers

Get started

The bottom number in a fraction tells you how many equal parts there are.

The top number tells you how many of those parts you are dealing with.

$\frac{1}{2}$ **of 8 is the same as 8 ÷ 2**

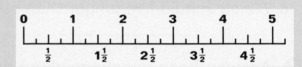

$\frac{1}{2}$ of 8 = 4

Fractions can also appear on number lines.

Halves are between whole numbers.

Quarters and three-quarters can also be on a number line.

```
 0       1       2       3       4       5
 |___|___|___|___|___|___|___|___|___|___|
     1/2     1 1/2   2 1/2   3 1/2   4 1/2
```

Practice

1 Write the answers.

a **Find $\frac{1}{2}$ of these.**

10 →
16 →
40 →
50 →
100 →

b **Find $\frac{1}{10}$ of these.**

30 →
40 →
60 →
90 →
100 →

c **Find $\frac{1}{5}$ of these.**

15 →
25 →
30 →
45 →
50 →

d **Find $\frac{1}{3}$ of these.**

12 →
15 →
21 →
24 →
30 →

2 Write the fraction each arrow points to.

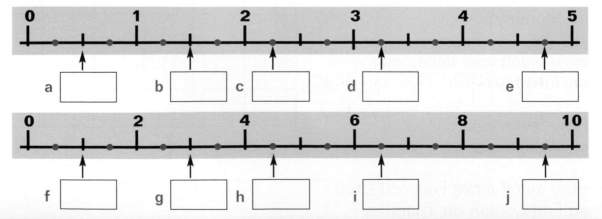

Challenge

3 Write the fraction of each set that is ringed.

a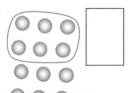

b

c

d

e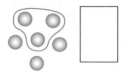

f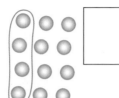

g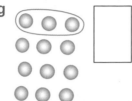

h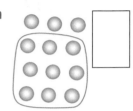

4 Answer these questions about the number line.

a Half-way between 2 and 3 is ☐   b Half-way between 0 and 1 is ☐

c Half-way between 1 and 3 is ☐   d Half-way between 0 and 4 is ☐

e Half-way between 0 and 3 is ☐   f Half-way between $\frac{1}{2}$ and 1 is ☐

g Half-way between 0 and $\frac{1}{2}$ is ☐   h Half-way between $1\frac{1}{2}$ and $2\frac{1}{2}$ is ☐

i Half-way between $2\frac{1}{2}$ and $3\frac{1}{2}$ is ☐   j Half-way between $4\frac{1}{2}$ and 5 is ☐

5 Write the answers.

a How many halves make a whole? ☐

b How many tenths make a whole? ☐

c How many quarters make a half? ☐

d How many tenths make a half? ☐

e How many quarters in 2 wholes? ☐

Topic 19

1 Multiply the number by 10.

$$(38) \longrightarrow \bigcirc$$

2 Divide the number by 10.

$$(700) \longrightarrow \bigcirc$$

3 Round the number to the nearest 10.

$$(74) \longrightarrow \bigcirc$$

4 Complete the table.

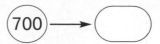

IN	2		5		9
OUT		400		700	

Topic 20

5 Tick the shape that has $\frac{1}{3}$ shaded.

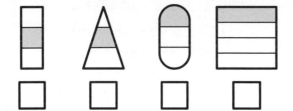

6 Write the fraction that is shaded.

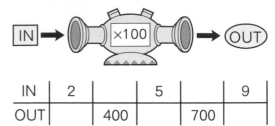

7 Tick the circle that has $\frac{3}{4}$ shaded.

8 Write the shaded fraction in two ways.

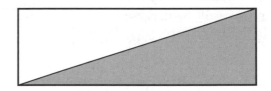

Topic 21

9 How many pennies is this?

£3.15 = ⬜ **p**

10 Write this amount in pounds.

204 p = £ ⬜

11 Write the total of these.

£1.70 and 90p = £ ⬜

12 I buy five tickets costing 50p each. How much change will I get from £5? **£** ⬜

Topic 22

13 Write how many ml.

1 litre and
200 millilitres = [   ] ml

14 Estimate and tick how much is in the jug.

[1000 ml jug]

50 ml   200 ml   500 ml

15 What is the reading?

[   ]

500 ml
400 ml
300 ml
200 ml
100 ml

16 What is the reading?

[   ]

1000 ml
800 ml
600 ml
400 ml
200 ml

Topic 23

17 How many visitors came to the school on Monday? [   ]

18 On which day were there 65 visitors? [   ]

19 How many more visited on Friday than on Tuesday? [   ]

20 Which day had ten more visitors than Thursday? [   ]

Visitors to school

Mon
Tue
Wed
Thur
Fri

0   10   20   30   40   50   60   70
number of people

Topic 24

21 What is a half of 50? [   ]

22 Which number does the arrow point to? [   ]

0   5

23 What fraction is ringed? [   ]

24 Which fraction is half-way between $\frac{1}{2}$ and 1? [   ]

Mark the test. Now add up all your test scores and put your final score on page 3.

Write your score out of 24. [   ]

Add a bonus point if you scored 20 or more.

TOTAL SCORE FOR TEST 4 [   ]

Answers

Topic 1: **Addition facts** (page 4)

1.

	a.	b.	c.	d.
	17	13	18	17
	12	14	17	18
	14	15	16	14
	12	13	20	20
	12	18	20	18
	16	12	17	19
	10	15	18	20
	11	10	16	19
	11	11	19	15
	11	16	18	20

2.

a.

+	3	7	8
4	7	11	12
6	9	13	14
8	11	15	16

b.

+	2	3	5
11	13	14	16
12	14	15	17
15	17	18	20

c.

+	12	13	14
4	16	17	18
5	17	18	19
6	18	19	20

3.

a. 4	b. 4	c. 7
d. 15	e. 6	f. 8
g. 7	h. 14	i. 6
j. 6	k. 5	l. 17
m. 9	n. 2	o. 9
p. 11	q. 9	r. 4
s. 5	t. 16	

4.

a. 12	b. 18	c. 13
d. 16	e. 20	f. 15
g. 14	h. 19	i. 20
j. 11	k. 19	l. 18
m. 12	n. 17	o. 17

5.

a.
IN	4	5	7	11	14
OUT	9	10	12	16	19

b.
IN	0	3	5	6	8
OUT	12	15	17	18	20

c. +4   d. +11

Topic 2: **Subtraction facts** (page 6)

1.

	a. 7	b. 8	c. 2	d. 8
	6	4	8	10
	7	9	8	7
	4	9	9	10
	4	9	9	7
	7	10	3	10
	6	8	4	9
	5	4	7	10
	7	6	6	6
	8	5	8	9

2.

a. 5	b. 7	c. 14	d. 8	e. 7
f. 16	g. 9	h. 4	i. 14	j. 7
k. 5	l. 14			

3.

a. 4	b. 3	c. 13	d. 17	e. 7
f. 8	g. 12	h. 17	i. 7	j. 2
k. 13	l. 19	m. 7	n. 7	o. 16
p. 19	q. 8	r. 2	s. 13	t. 20

4.

a. 7	b. 10	c. 7	d. 9	e. 11
f. 5	g. 8	h. 15	i. 3	j. 9
k. 16	l. 6	m. 6	n. 13	o. 6

5.

a. + −	b. − +	c. + −	d. − +	e. + −
f. + −	g. + +	h. − −	i. + −	

Topic 3: **Place value** (page 8)

1.

a. 850	b. 1200
c. 303	d. 3080
e. 967	f. 6012
g. 515	h. 7004
i. 725	j. 9236

2.

a. 478	b. 232
c. 797	d. 145
e. 833	f. 556
g. 921	h. 314

3.

a. 400 + 30 + 6	b. 100 + 80 + 4
c. 600 + 60 + 2	d. 700 + 10 + 5
e. 900 + 30 + 8	f. 500 + 40 + 1
g. 200 + 50 + 3	h. 800 + 90 + 7

4.

a. 70	b. 400	c. 2	d. 30	e. 50	f. 4000
g. 300	h. 60	i. 80	j. 4000	k. 9	k. 7000

5.

a.	105	150	501	505	510	550
b.	367	376	637	673	736	763
c.	238	283	328	382	823	832
d.	1234	1432	3124	3421	4123	
e.	2074	2407	2704	4270	7024	
f.	1002	1020	1200	2010	2100	

6.

457	475	547	574	745	754

Topic 4: **Counting** (page 10)

1.

a. 40	b. 72	c. 54	d. 85
e. 38	f. 59	g. 64	h. 78
i. 131	j. 191	k. 611	l. 804
m. 169	n. 505	o. 637	p. 799

2.

a. 7	b. 87	c. 68
3	103	83
7	295	295
6	707	436

3.

a.	46	56	66	+10
b.	45	49	53	+4
c.	84	79	74	−5
d.	49	58	67	+9
e.	56	47	38	−9

4.

a. IN	49	65	116	194	304
b. IN	53	102	184	301	610
c. IN	46	63	201	435	719
d. IN	51	75	313	622	829

Topic 5: **2D shapes** (page 12)

1.

a. rectangle or quadrilateral	b. triangle	c. pentagon
d. oval	e. pentagon	f. quadrilateral
g. hexagon	h. triangle	i. semi-circle
j. pentagon	k. quadrilateral	l. triangle
m. triangle	n. quadrilateral	o. hexagon

2.

a. quadrilateral	b. hexagon	c. pentagon

3.

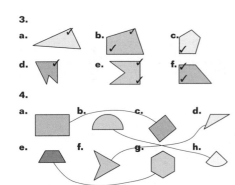

4.

a. b. c. d.
e. f. g. h.

(shapes connected with lines)

● Topic 6: **Time** (page 14)

1.
a. 1:15
b. 5:55
c. 10:35
d. 7:25
e. 12:10
f. 9:05
g. 2:20
h. 4:45

2.

a b c d

3:10 **9:55** **6:05** **12:20**

3.
a. 30   b. 15
c. 45   d. 24 hours
e. 52   f. September
g. March   h. 30
i. 30   j. 366

4.
a. 15
b. 25
c. 25
d. 50

5.
a. 3·45
b. 7:55
c. 3:25
d. 6:40
e. 11:40

● Test 1 (page 16)

1. 7   **2.** 18   **3.** 7 8   **4.** 9
5. 20   **6.** 8   **7.** 13   **8.** 15
9. three thousand and five   **10.** 607 660 670 706 760 770
11. 500   **12.** 258   **13.** 291   **14.** 367
15. 6   **16.** 43,49,55 **17.** quadrilateral **18.** hexagon
19.   **20.**   **21.** 2:40   **22.** 4:25
23. 31   **24.** 60

● Topic 7: **Addition** (page 18)

1.
a. 79   b. 57   c. 79   d. 88
e. 60   f. 60   g. 90   h. 80
i. 71   j. 92   k. 91   l. 82

2.
a. 124   b. 121   c. 176   d. 132   e. 133

3.

a.
18	24	**42**
16	26	**42**
34	**50**	**84**

b.
26	34	**60**
14	27	**41**
40	**61**	**101**

c.
19	26	**45**
37	34	**71**
56	**60**	**116**

d.
27	36	**63**
18	28	**46**
45	**64**	**109**

4.
a. 4   b. 1   c. 5   d. 3   e. 6
f. 5   g. 6   h. 8   i. 9   j. 7

5.
26 and 24   19 and 31   17 and 33   27 and 23

6.
a. 66
b. 51
c. 38 28 24
d. 35 24 16
e. 141

● Topic 8: **Subtraction** (page 20)

1.
a. 34   b. 22   c. 56   d. 30   e. 15   f. 32
g. 33   h. 34   i. 24   j. 26   k. 37   l. 27

2.
a. 36   b. 27   c. 28   d. 35   e. 27

3.

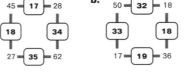

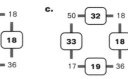

a.
```
45 —[17]— 28
[18]      [34]
27 —[35]— 62
```
b.
```
50 —[32]— 18
[33]      [18]
17 —[19]— 36
```
c.
```
50 —[32]— 18
[33]      [18]
17 —[19]— 36
```

4.
a. 7   b. 5   c. 6   d. 5   e. 9
f. 4   g. 4   h. 5   i. 6   j. 3

5.
a. 81 62 43 24
b. 85 69 52 34
c. 77 61 38 22

6.
a. 15
b. 20
c. C (57)
d. D and F (48, 28)
e. B and D (76, 48)

● Topic 9: **Symmetry** (page 22)

1.
a and **f** have two options
a.   b.   c.
d.   e.   f.
g.   h.

2. E

3.
a.   b.   c.
d.   e.   f.

4.
a.   b.   c.
d.   e.   f.

5. HAT
BEE
Check that the words made up are symmetrical.

Topic 10: **Sequence and patterns** (page 24)

1.

a. △□□△□□△□□

b. ○□▽○□▽○□▽

c. 7 7 4 7 7 4 **7 7 4**

d. 1 2 3 3 2 1 **1 2 3**

e. |○∞|○∞|○∞

f. (=)(=) (=)

3.

a.	107	123	141	159		
	130	142	168	174		
b.	25	35	40	60	95	
	38	52	74			
c.	28	50	58	62		
	17	31	37	45		
d.	10	50	60	80	90	100
	15	45				

2.

a.	72	82	92
b.	20	15	10
c.	33	35	37
d.	68	66	64
e.	42	46	50

4.

a.	85	80	75
b.	91	88	85
c.	70	60	50

5.

a. 301	b. 600
c. 80	d. 130
e. 36	f. 36

Topic 11: **Position, direction and angles** (page 26)

1.

a. E	b. S
c. W	d. W
e. N	f. N
g. S	h. S
i. N	j. E
k. N	l. E

2.
a. b. c. d. e. f.

3.

a. swing
b. see-saw
c. kite
d. see-saw
e. swing

4.

N

Topic 12: **Length** (page 28)

1.

a. 200 cm	b. 120 cm	c. 245 cm	d. 500 cm
e. 177 cm	f. 305 cm	g. 50 cm	h. 304 cm
i. 550 cm	j. 350 cm	k. 529 cm	l. 832 cm

2.

a. 4.70 m	b. 1.25 m	c. 3.70 m	d. 6.15 m
e. 8.35 m	f. 2.80 m	g. 1.10 m	h. 4.90 m
i. 7.50 m	j. 8.95 m		

3.

a. 65 cm	b. 45 cm	c. 15 cm	d. 85 cm
e. 36 cm	f. 68 cm	g. 4 cm	h. 83 cm

4.

a. 2.75 m
b. 1.75 m
c. 1.6 m
d. 1.5 m
e. 1.3 m

5.

a. 1 cm
b. 4 cm
c. 8 cm
d. 14 cm

6.

a. $3\frac{1}{2}$ cm
b. $7\frac{1}{2}$ cm
c. $10\frac{1}{2}$ cm
d. 13 cm

Test 2 (page 30)

1. 87	**2.** 122	**3.** 5	**4.** 55
5. 42	**6.** 26	**7.** 2	**8.** 27

9. **10.** **11.** **12.** N

13. 28	**14.** 45	**15.** 732	**16.** 300
17. West	**18.**	**19.**	**20.**

21. 250 cm	**22.** 375 cm	**23.** 55 cm	**24.** 1.2 m

Topic 13: **Addition and subtraction** (page 32)

1.

a. 74	b. 28	c. 60	d. 45	e. 91
f. 11	g. 92	h. 26	i. 84	j. 45

2.

a. 44	b. 54
c. 31	d. 87
e. 85	f. 12
g. 15	h. 75

3.

a. 83	46	74
b. 66	81	54
c. 90	53	18
d. 47	30	5
e. 22	60	89

4.

a. 7 b. 8 c. 2 d. 0 e. 5
f. 6 g. 4 h. 1 i. 3 j. 4 4

5.

a. 153 b. 16 c. 55 36
d. 72 17 e. 36 39

Topic 14: **Multiplication** (page 34)

1.

a. 4	b. 25	c. 50	d. 15	e. 20
6	10	20	6	8
14	35	70	21	28
20	50	100	30	40
16	40	80	24	32
18	45	90	27	36
12	30	60	18	24
8	20	40	12	16
10	6	30	9	12
0	0	0	0	0

2.

a.

×	4	7	9
2	8	14	18
5	20	35	45
10	40	70	90

b.

×	3	6	8
2	6	12	16
5	15	30	40
10	30	60	80

c.

×	4	7	8
3	12	21	24
4	16	28	32
5	20	35	40

3.

a.	IN	2	**4**	5	**7**	8
	OUT	**4**	8	**10**	14	**16**
b.	IN	3	**5**	6	**7**	9
	OUT	**15**	25	**30**	35	**45**
c.	IN	2	**4**	5	**7**	10
	OUT	**6**	12	**15**	21	**30**
d.	IN	4	**5**	7	**9**	10
	OUT	**16**	20	**28**	36	**40**

4.
Any four from:
a. 1×12 2×6 3×4 4×3 6×2 12×1
b. 1×18 2×9 9×2 6×3 3×6 18×1
c. 1×24 4×6 6×4 8×3 3×8 2×12 12×2 24×1
d. 1×30 2×15 15×2 3×10 10×3 5×6 6×5 30×1

5.
(Other answers are possible.)
a. 3×5 9×2 3×4 7×3 8×2 4×5 7×5
b. 2×4 9×5 10×5 7×2 6×4 8×4 9×4

Topic 15: **3D Shapes** (page 36)

1.
a. sphere
b. triangular prism
c. cone
d. hexagonal prism
e. cuboid
f. hemisphere
g. cube
h. cylinder
i. triangular prism
j. pentagonal prism
k. cylinder
l. cuboid

2.
a. 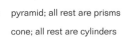 triangular prism; all rest have a circle in their cross-section, or have a curved surface
b. hemisphere; all the rest are prisms
c. pyramid; all rest are prisms
d. cone; all rest are cylinders

3.
a. sometimes
b. always
c. never
d. always
e. sometimes

Topic 16: **Weight and mass** (page 38)

	1.	2.	3.	4.	5.
a.	2000 g	2	500 g	300 g	$1\frac{1}{2}$ kg
b.	5000 g	5	1500 g	700 g	4 kg
c.	3000 g	10	2500 g	200 g	$5\frac{1}{2}$ kg
d.	6000 g	20		300 g	$2\frac{1}{2}$ kg
e.	500 g	5		300 g	
f.	1500 g	10			

Topic 17: **Charts and diagrams** (page 40)

1.

	odd numbers	not odd numbers
multiples of 5	15 35	20 30
not multiples of 5	13 21	14 24

2.

3.
a.

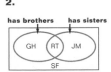

	can eat the peel	cannot eat the peel
has pips	apple	orange lemon
does not have pips	plum peach cherry	banana

4.
even numbers → 24 40 32
numbers ending in 0 → 40 70
25 35

One loop is completely inside the other because all numbers that end with 0 are even numbers.

Topic 18: **Division** (page 42)

1.
a. 6 **b.** 10 **c.** 8 **d.** 4
e. 7 **f.** 9 **g.** 3 **h.** 8
i. 7 **j.** 7

2.
a. 7 **b.** 10 **c.** 6 **d.** 5
e. 8 **f.** 3 **g.** 2 **h.** 5
i. 9 **j.** 8

3.
a. 7 **b.** 3 **c.** 4 **d.** 6
e. 9 **f.** 9 **g.** 6 **h.** 8

4.
a. 8 **b.** 9 **c.** 6 **d.** 7
e. 20 **f.** 30 **g.** 40 **h.** 10
i. 15 **j.** 25 **k.** 35 **l.** 45

5.

a. IN	6	8	12	16	20
OUT	3	4	6	8	10
b. IN	10	20	25	40	45
OUT	2	4	5	8	9
c. IN	6	12	18	24	27
OUT	2	4	6	8	9
d. IN	12	16	24	32	40
OUT	3	4	6	8	10

6.
a. 10 6 **b.** 5 2 **c.** 8 6 **d.** 9 6
e. 10 5 **f.** 20 10 **g.** 40 8 **h.** 50 10

Test 3 (page 44)

1.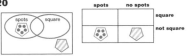
2. 7 3
3. 73
4. 61
5. 5
6. 6
7. 14p
8. 14 12 21 25
9. hemisphere
10. triangular prism
11. hexagonal prism
12. cuboid
13. 4
14. 1 kg and 200 g
15. 160 kg
16. $4\frac{1}{2}$ g
17–20

	spots	no spots	
square			square
			not square

21. 7
22. 18
23. 7
24. 50

Topic 19: **Tens and hundreds** (page 46)

1.
a. 150 **b.** 590
c. 180 **d.** 650
e. 200 **f.** 710
g. 12 **h.** 57
i. 23 **j.** 60
k. 30 **l.** 79

2.
a. 50 **b.** 70
c. 50 **d.** 90
e. 60 **f.** 100
g. 200 **h.** 600
i. 400 **j.** 600
k. 400 **l.** 1000

3.

a.
(35) (43) (56) (75) (84)
| 0 10 20 30 40 50 60 70 80 90 100 |
(22) (31) (47) (68) (95)

b.
(275) (422) (551) (693) (762)
| 0 100 200 300 400 500 600 700 800 900 1000 |
(350) (505) (639) (747) (949)

4.

a. IN	11	16	22	35	60
OUT	110	160	220	350	600
b. IN	40	120	370	420	750
OUT	4	12	37	42	75

5.
< 345 > < 472 > < 454 > < 538 > < 591 >
| 300   400   500   600 |

Topic 20: **Fractions and shapes** (page 48)

1.
a. $\frac{1}{4}$ **b.** $\frac{2}{6}$ or $\frac{1}{3}$
c. $\frac{1}{4}$ **d.** $\frac{1}{2}$
e. $\frac{1}{4}$ **f.** $\frac{1}{2}$
g. $\frac{1}{3}$ **h.** $\frac{1}{2}$
i. $\frac{1}{4}$ **j.** $\frac{2}{8}$ or $\frac{1}{4}$

2.
a. $\frac{2}{8}$ or $\frac{1}{4}$ **b.** $\frac{2}{6}$ or $\frac{1}{3}$
c. $\frac{3}{6}$ or $\frac{1}{2}$ **d.** $\frac{2}{8}$ or $\frac{1}{4}$
e. $\frac{2}{6}$ or $\frac{1}{3}$ **f.** $\frac{2}{4}$ or $\frac{1}{2}$
g. $\frac{4}{8}$ or $\frac{1}{2}$ **h.** $\frac{2}{8}$ or $\frac{1}{4}$
i. $\frac{2}{6}$ or $\frac{1}{3}$ **j.** $\frac{2}{16}$ or $\frac{1}{8}$

3.
a. $\frac{2}{4}$ and $\frac{1}{2}$ **b.** $\frac{2}{6}$ and $\frac{1}{3}$
c. $\frac{3}{9}$ and $\frac{1}{3}$ **d.** $\frac{2}{8}$ and $\frac{1}{4}$
e. $\frac{3}{12}$ and $\frac{1}{4}$ **f.** $\frac{6}{12}$ and $\frac{1}{2}$

4.
a. $\frac{1}{3}$ **b.** $\frac{1}{4}$
c. $\frac{1}{5}$ **d.** $\frac{1}{8}$
e. $\frac{3}{4}$ **f.** $\frac{2}{3}$
g. $\frac{7}{8}$ **h.** $\frac{4}{5}$

5.
a. $\frac{1}{4}$ **b.** $\frac{1}{3}$
c. $\frac{1}{2}$ **d.** $\frac{2}{3}$
e. $\frac{3}{4}$

Topic 21: **Money** (page 50)

1.
a. 3p
7p
5p
8p
b. 10p
5p
9p
3p
c. 40p
30p
45p
38p
d. 80p
50p
90p
95p

2.
a. 145p **b.** 401p
c. 205p **d.** 618p
e. 395p **f.** 879p
g. £1.20 **h.** £5.18
i. £2.25 **j.** £6.72
k. £3.05 **l.** £9.34

3.
a. £1.50 **b.** £3.50 **c.** £1.50 **d.** £2.70
e. £1.75 **f.** £3.25 **g.** £1.40 **h.** £2.70
i. £1.05 **j.** £7.50 **k.** £1.20 **l.** £3.00

4.
a. £3.50
b. £2.50
c. 75p
d. 9 cans
e. £1.75

5.
a. £1 and 50p
b. £2 and £1
c. £2 and 20p
d. 50p and 20p

Topic 22: **Capacity** (page 52)

1.
a. 2000 ml **b.** 5000 ml **c.** 3000 ml **d.** 6000 ml
e. 500 ml **f.** 1500 ml **g.** 3500 ml **h.** 2500 ml

2.
a. 2
b. 4
c. 10
d. 20
e. 20

3.
a. 100 ml
b. 50 ml
c. 90 ml

4.
a. 500 ml
b. 750 ml
c. 400 ml
d. 5
e. 2

5.
a. 2 l
b. 1 l
c. 3 l
d. 4 l

Topic 23: **Graphs** (page 54)

1.
a. 6
b. 7
c. 13
d. 8:00
e. 7:30

2.
a. 9
b. 8
c. 3
d. football
e. reading
f. swimming

3.
a. cat
b. 40 years
c. elephant
d. human
and
elephant

4.
a. coffee
b. cola
c. 8
d. 7
e. 4

5.
a. £1.00
b. £1.50
c. £2.10
d. £1.90
e. £1.00

Topic 24: **Fractions and numbers** (page 56)

1.
a. 5	**b.** 3	**c.** 3	**d.** 4
8	4	5	5
20	6	6	7
25	9	9	8
50	10	10	10

2.
a. $\frac{1}{2}$ **b.** $1\frac{1}{2}$ **c.** $2\frac{1}{4}$ **d.** $3\frac{1}{4}$ **e.** $4\frac{3}{4}$
f. 1 **g.** 3 **h.** $4\frac{1}{2}$ **i.** $6\frac{1}{2}$ **j.** $9\frac{1}{2}$

3.
a. $\frac{3}{6}$ or $\frac{1}{2}$ **b.** $\frac{2}{6}$ or $\frac{1}{3}$ **c.** $\frac{2}{8}$ or $\frac{1}{4}$ **d.** $\frac{4}{8}$ or $\frac{1}{2}$
e. $\frac{6}{12}$ or $\frac{1}{2}$ **f.** $\frac{4}{12}$ or $\frac{1}{3}$ **g.** $\frac{3}{12}$ or $\frac{1}{4}$ **h.** $\frac{9}{12}$ or $\frac{3}{4}$

4.
a. $2\frac{1}{2}$ **b.** $\frac{1}{2}$
c. 2 **d.** 2
e. $\frac{1}{2}$ **f.** $\frac{3}{4}$
g. $\frac{1}{4}$ **h.** 2
i. 3 **j.** $4\frac{3}{4}$

5.
a. 2
b. 10
c. 2
d. 5
e. 8

Test 4 (page 58)

1. 380 **2.** 70 **3.** 70

4.
IN	2	4	5	7	9
OUT	200	400	500	700	900

5 [shapes row with first box ticked ✓]

6. $\frac{1}{2}$

7. [circles row with first circle ticked ✓]

8. $\frac{2}{3}$ and $\frac{4}{6}$

9. 315p **10.** £2.04 **11.** £2.60
12. £2.50 **13.** 1200 ml **14.** 200 ml
15. 250 ml **16.** 300 ml **17.** 45
18. Wednesday **19.** 25 **20.** Monday
21. 25 **22.** $3\frac{1}{2}$ **23.** $\frac{2}{8}$ or $\frac{1}{4}$
24. $\frac{3}{4}$